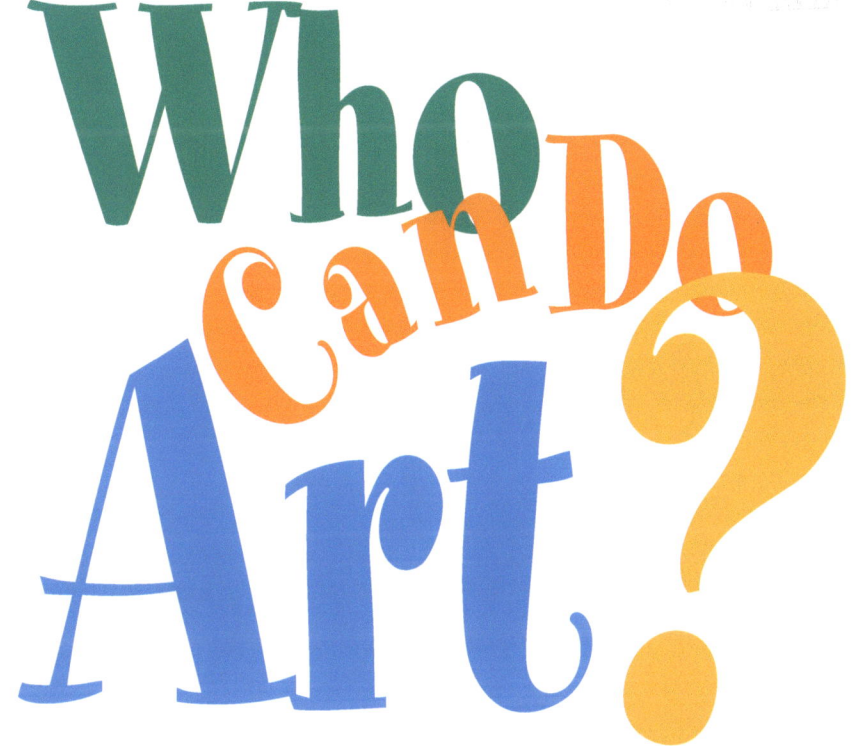

Who Can Do Art?

Written by

Cristina Barnes

Designed by

Adrienne Beaver

GPUB01371-00001
Who Can Do Art?
1-4196-0098-2
Pub Date: Jul-15-2004

This book is dedicated to my mother,
whose insight, encouragement, and love impact every aspect of my life.

I would like to acknowledge and thank the following artists
who have inspired me with their creativity.
It is their artwork that makes this book special, and I hope their many talents
will help young readers realize their own artistic abilities.

Adrienne Beaver

James Dippery

Bill Lynch

Alison Thomas

Jack Barnes

Shannon Hackenberg

Jennifer Dippery

Kate Thomas

Joey Barnes

Jeff Keiffer

Connor Beaver

Eliot Beaver

and most of all, Nathan Korn, who thought he hated art.

Special thanks to my sister Andi, who not only designed the layout, created the
fashion design, and produced the print-ready output...she also listened, prompted,
advised, encouraged, reminded, and just supported me every step of the way.

an Artist

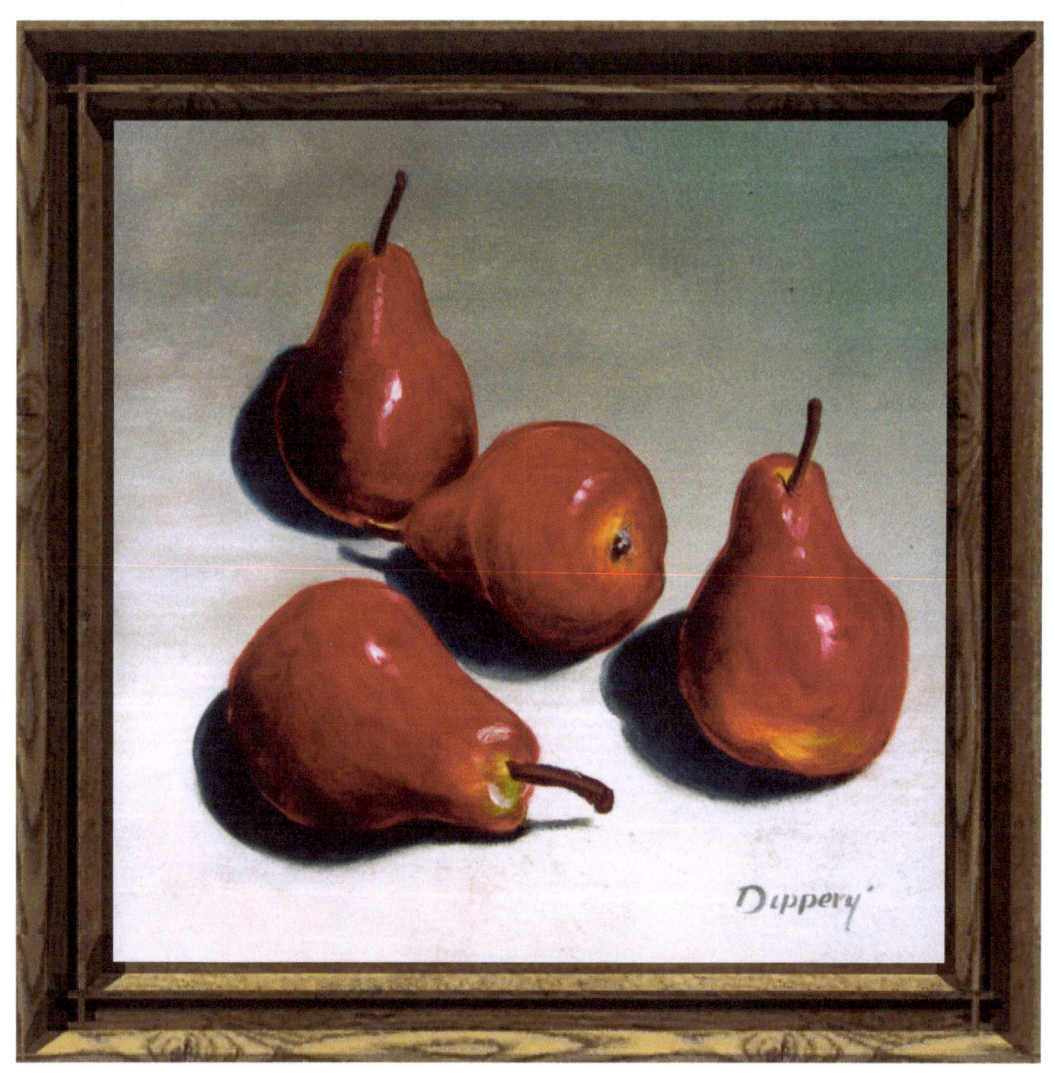

Art is a painting, colorful and real.

a Potter

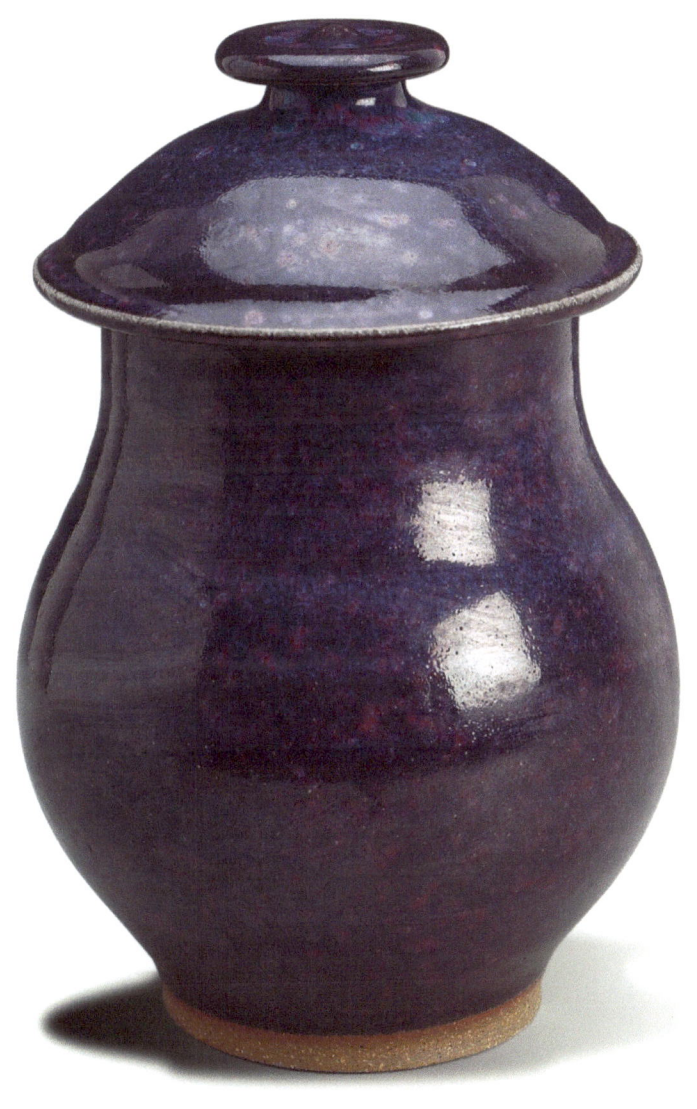

It's also a pot, spun on a wheel.

Art is a pirouette,
at the end of the dance.

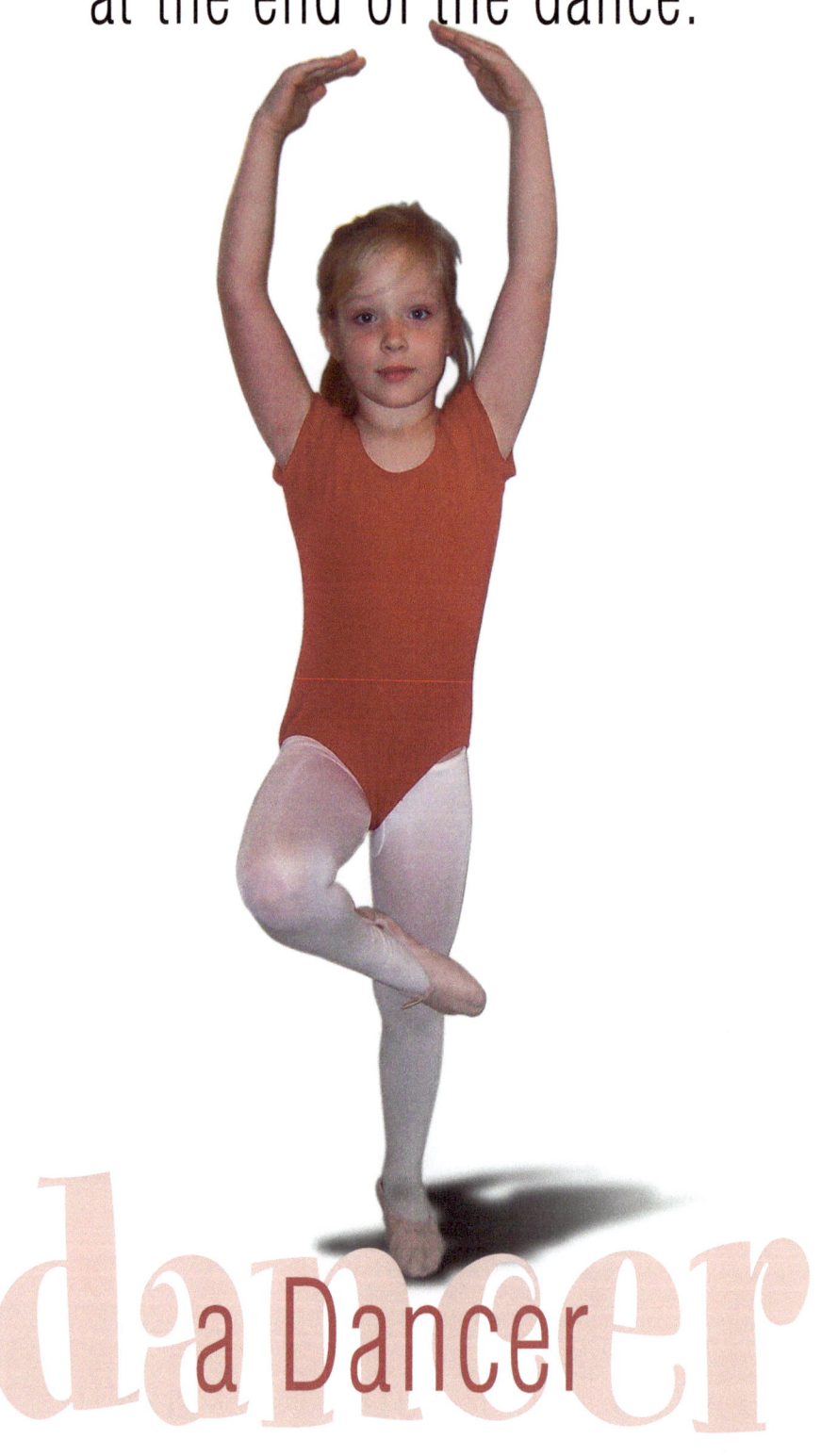

a Dancer

a Fashion Designer

A designer's vision of a shirt and pants.

Art is a poem, rhyming or not... or a well-told story with characters and plot.

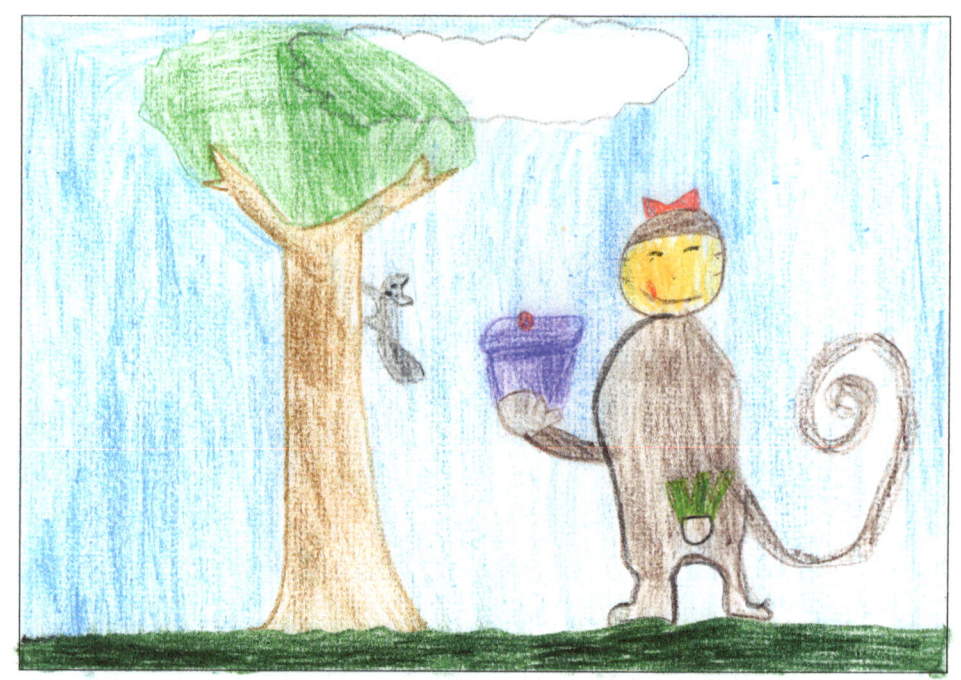

There's an M on my Muffin

One gloomy day, Maggie the monkey bought herself a muffin. She paid for it with her own money. It looked scrumptious. It was a huge muffin, the biggest she'd ever had!

In fact, it was monstrous.[1]

_____

[1] **Monstrous** means really big, as in: "Wow, that's a monstrous muffin, or that's a monstrous monster."

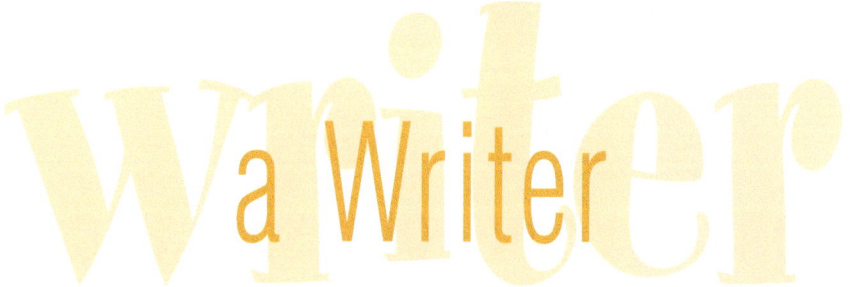

You!

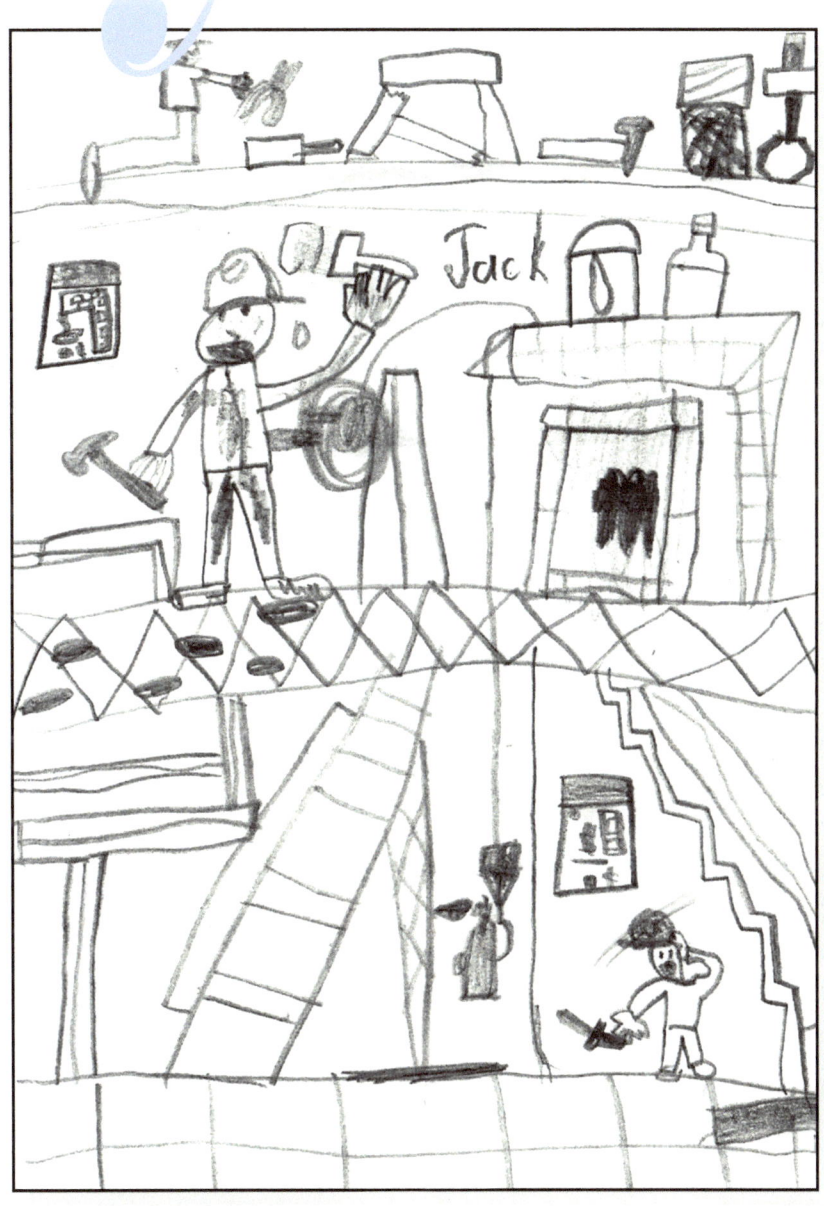

Art is the picture you drew on paper
for Mommy to hang on the refrigerator.

a Musician

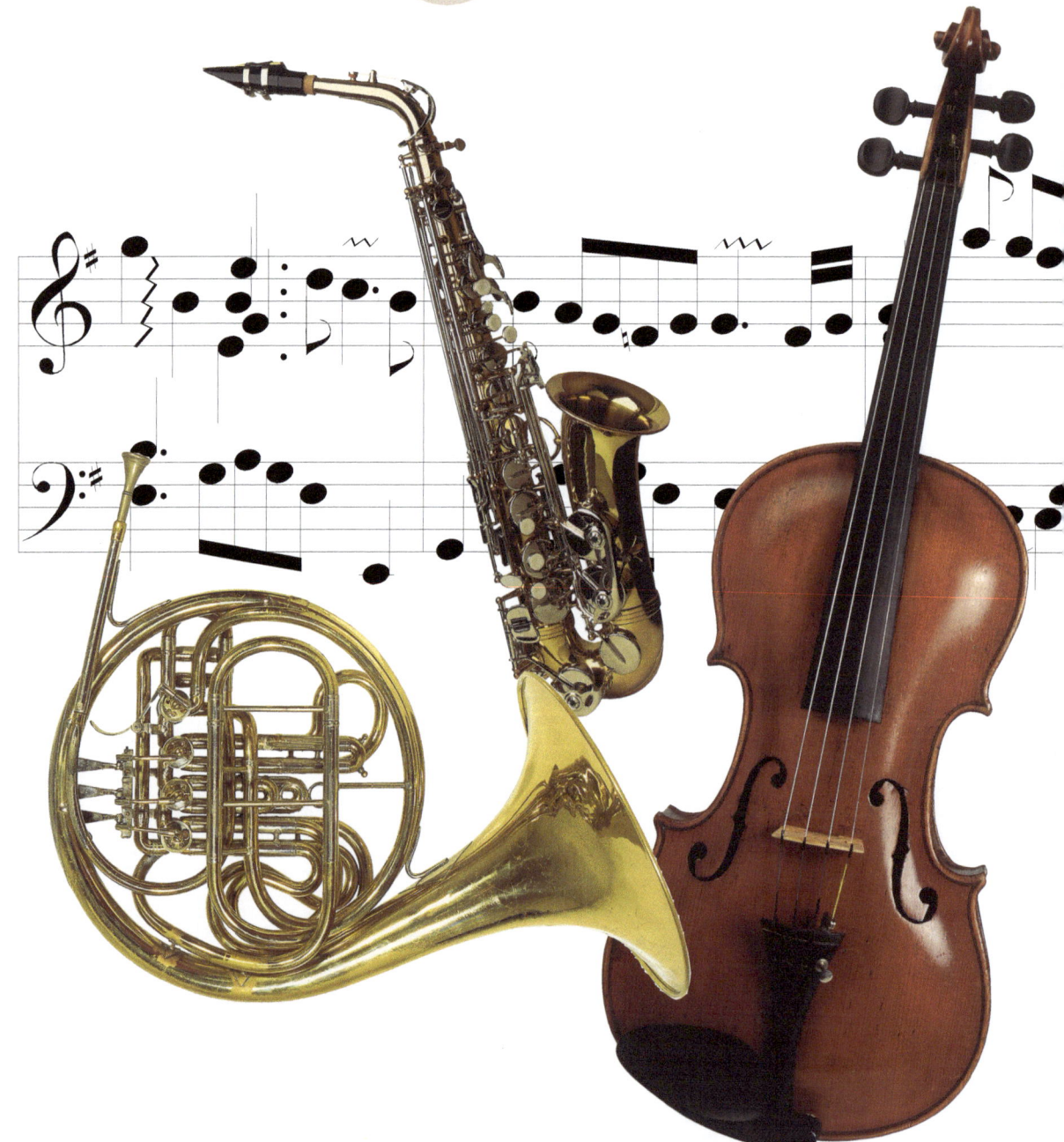

Art is a rhapsody — splendid and loud!

or a symbol of freedom, tall and proud.

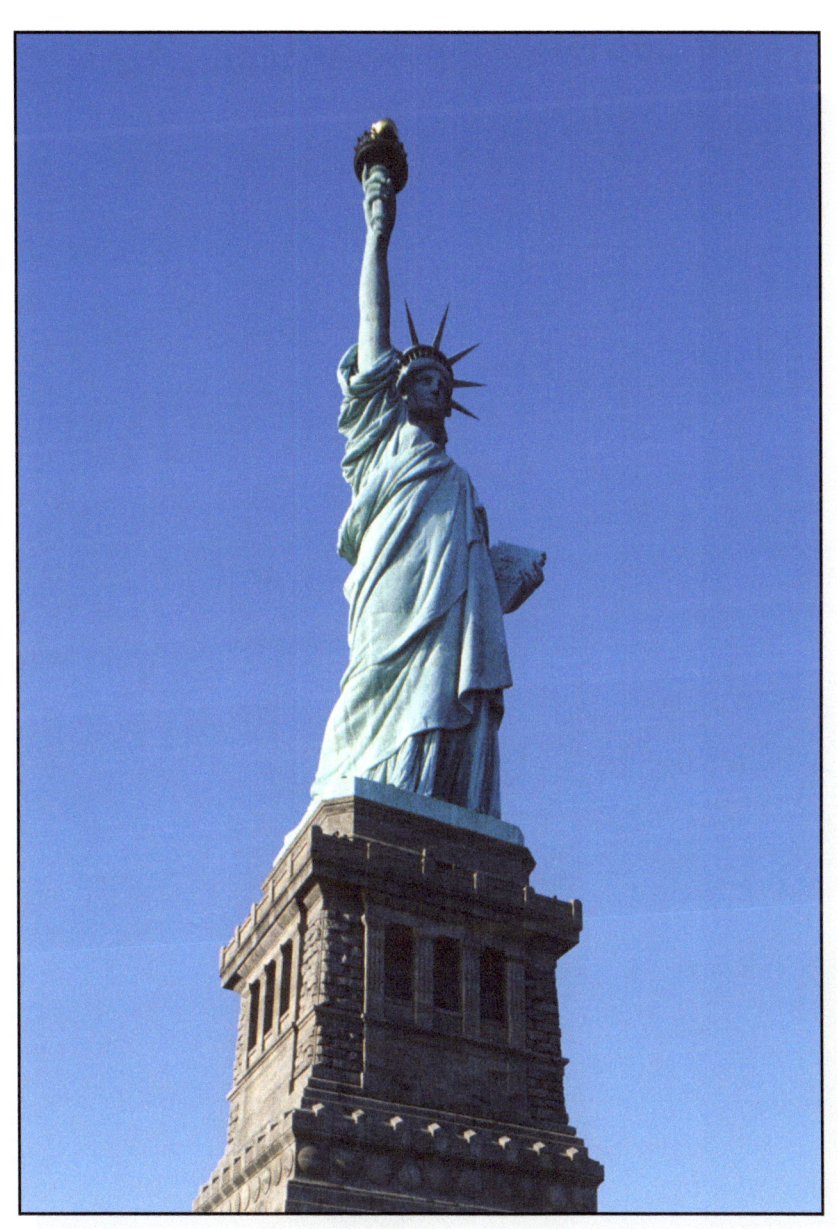

a Sculptor

a Landscaper

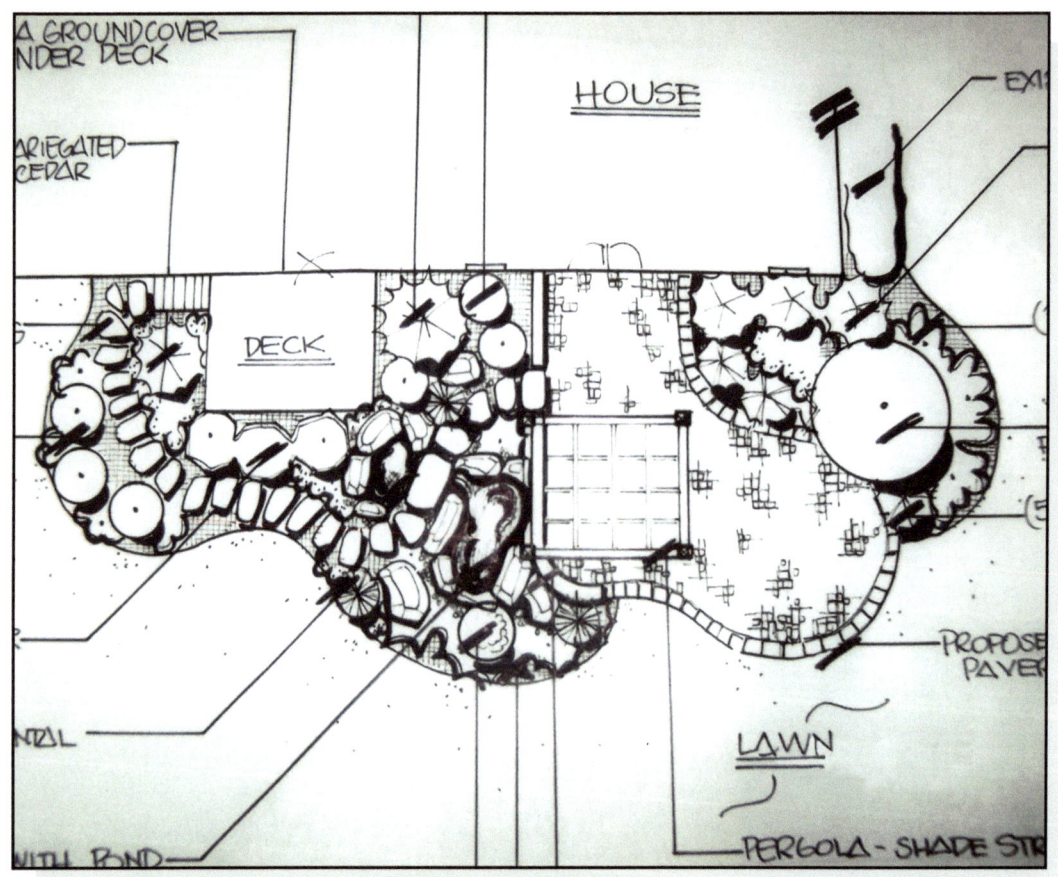

Art is designing a natural show...

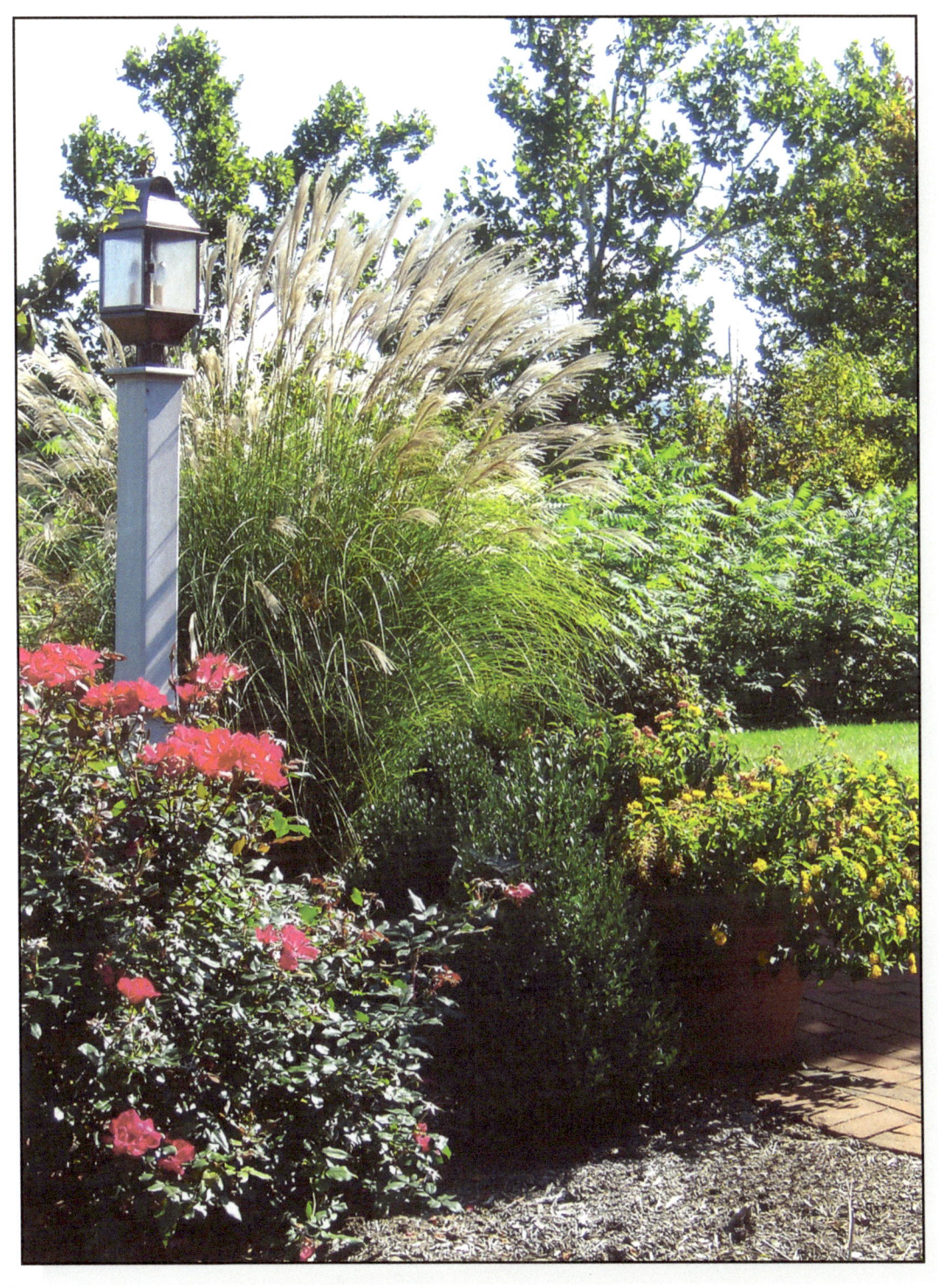

that springs to life with shovel and hoe.

Art is a horseshoe
hammered from metal.

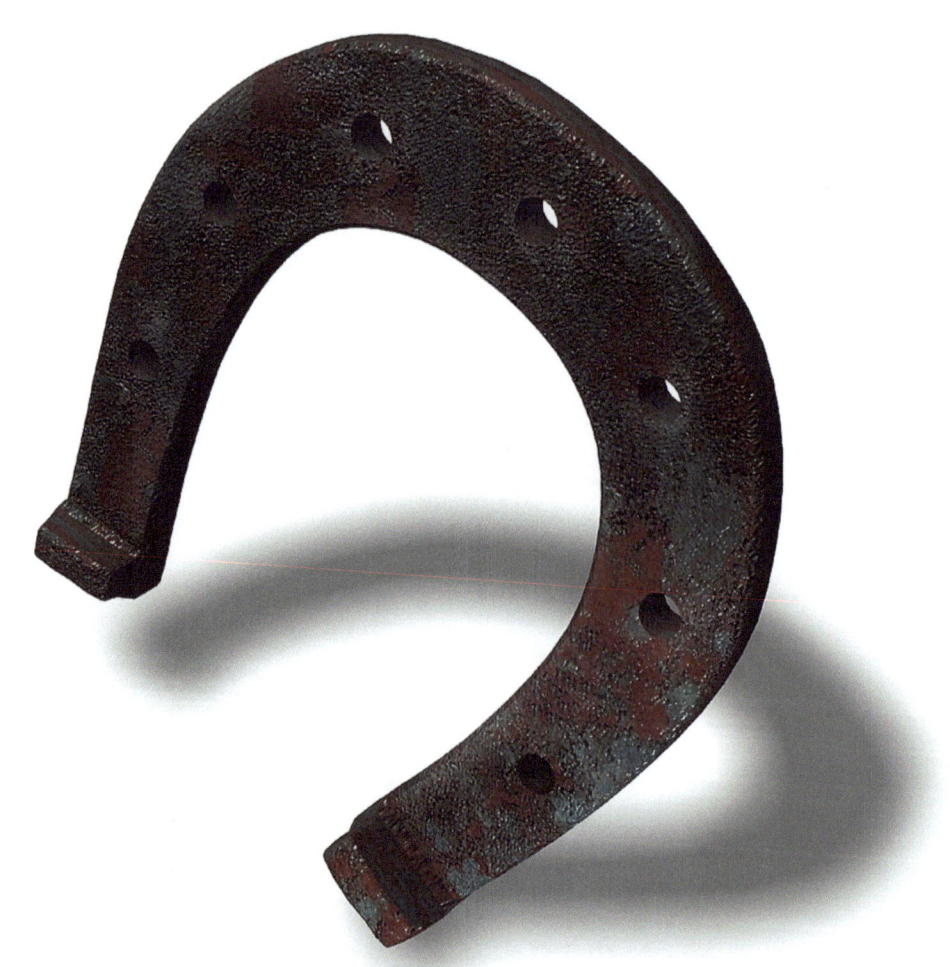

a Blacksmith

a Photographer

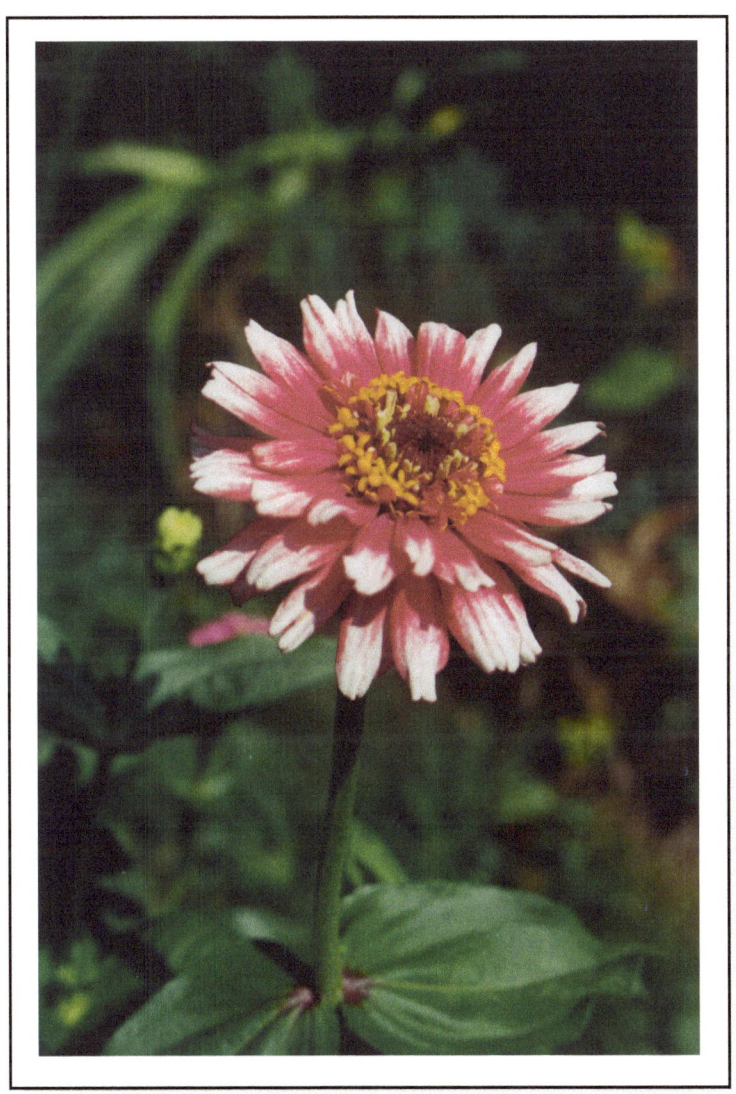

Art is a photograph
of a flower petal.

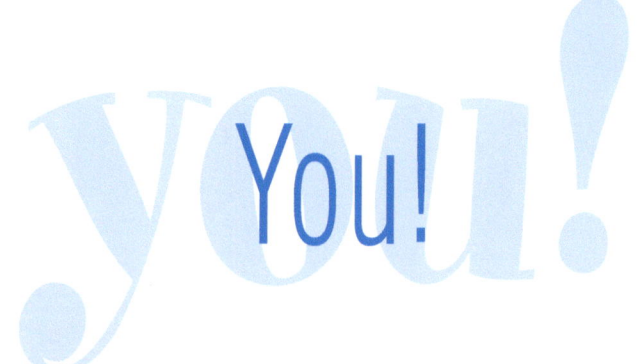

You!

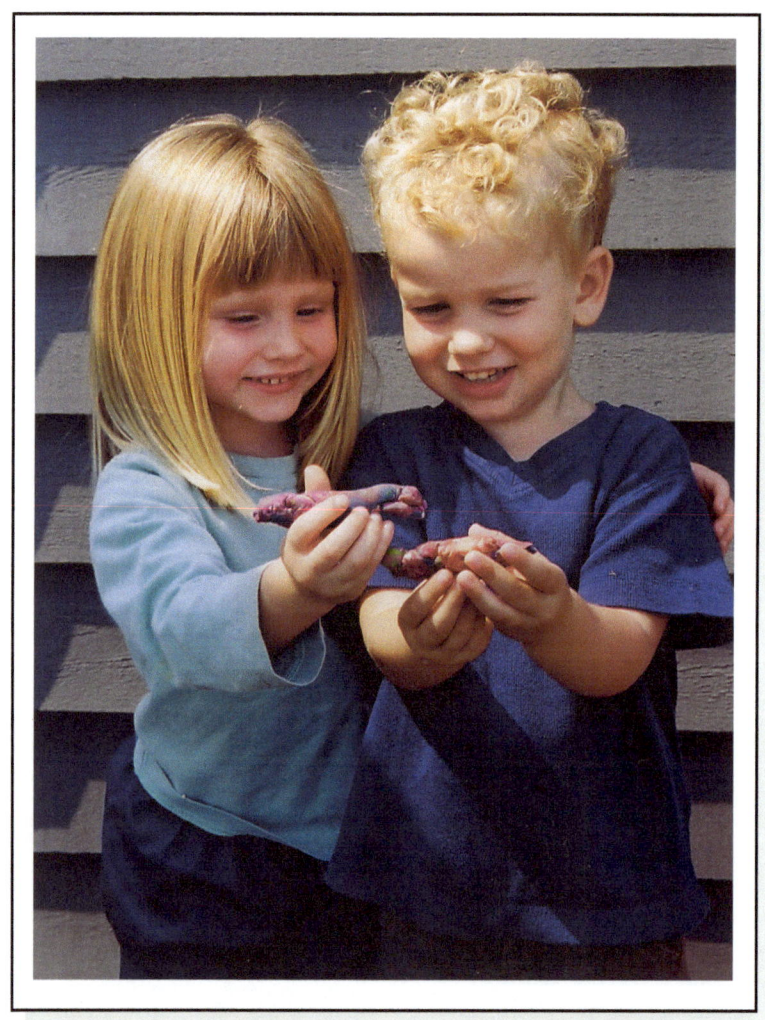

Art is the snake
you sculpted from clay,

Did I mention that
YOU can do art?

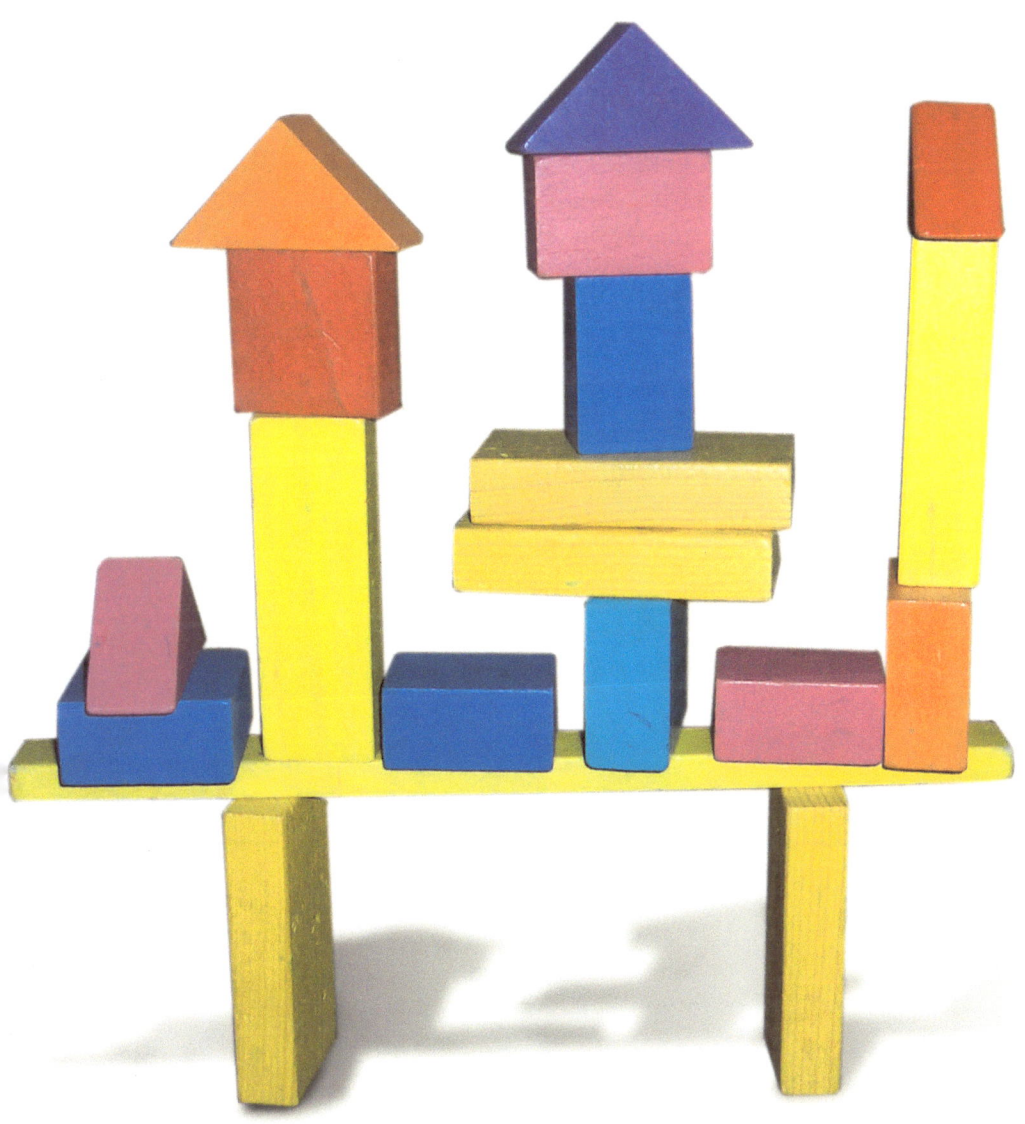

and the tower you made
with blocks yesterday.

Art is a computer aided design,

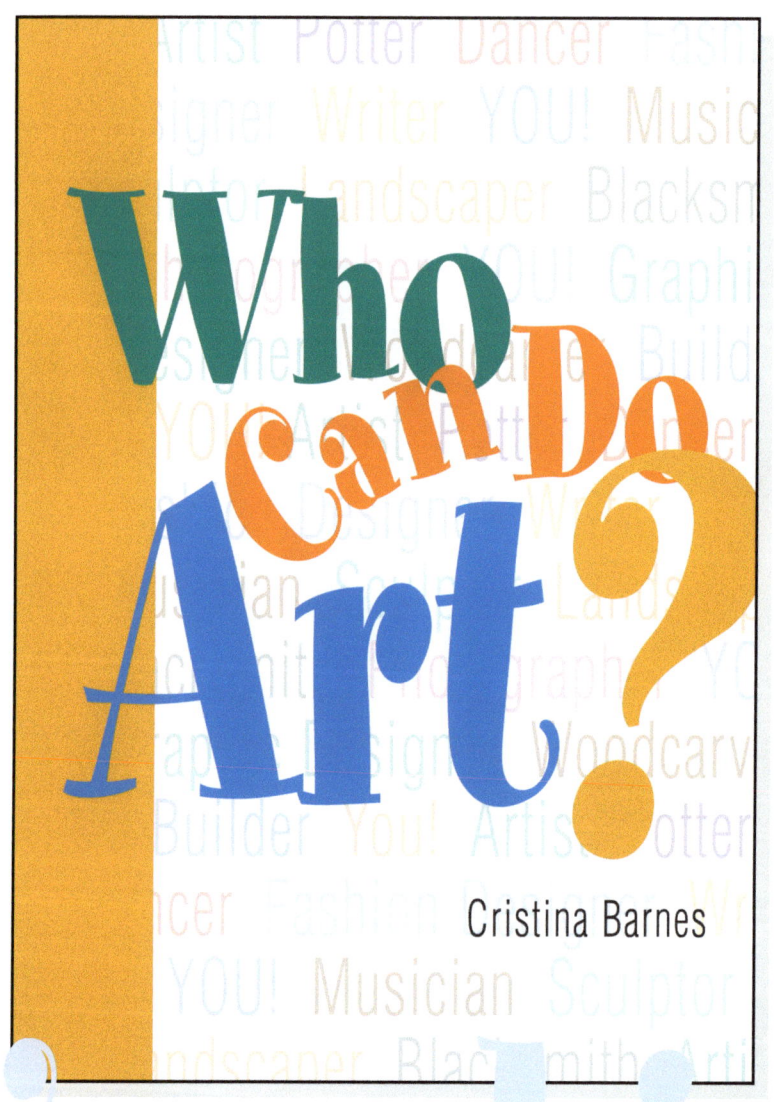

Who Can Do Art?

Cristina Barnes

a Graphic Designer

a Woodcarver

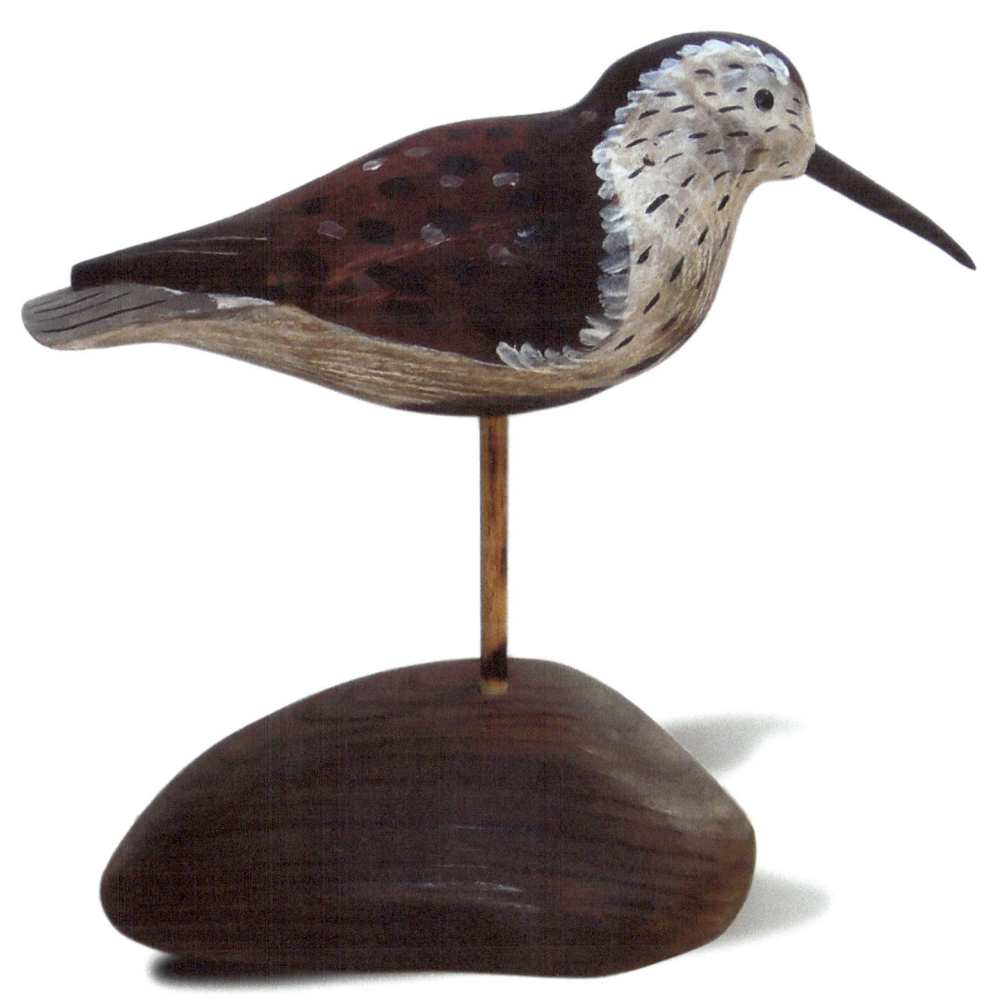

or a wooden bird carved out of pine.

Art is a castle, regal and grand — built from stone and mortar...

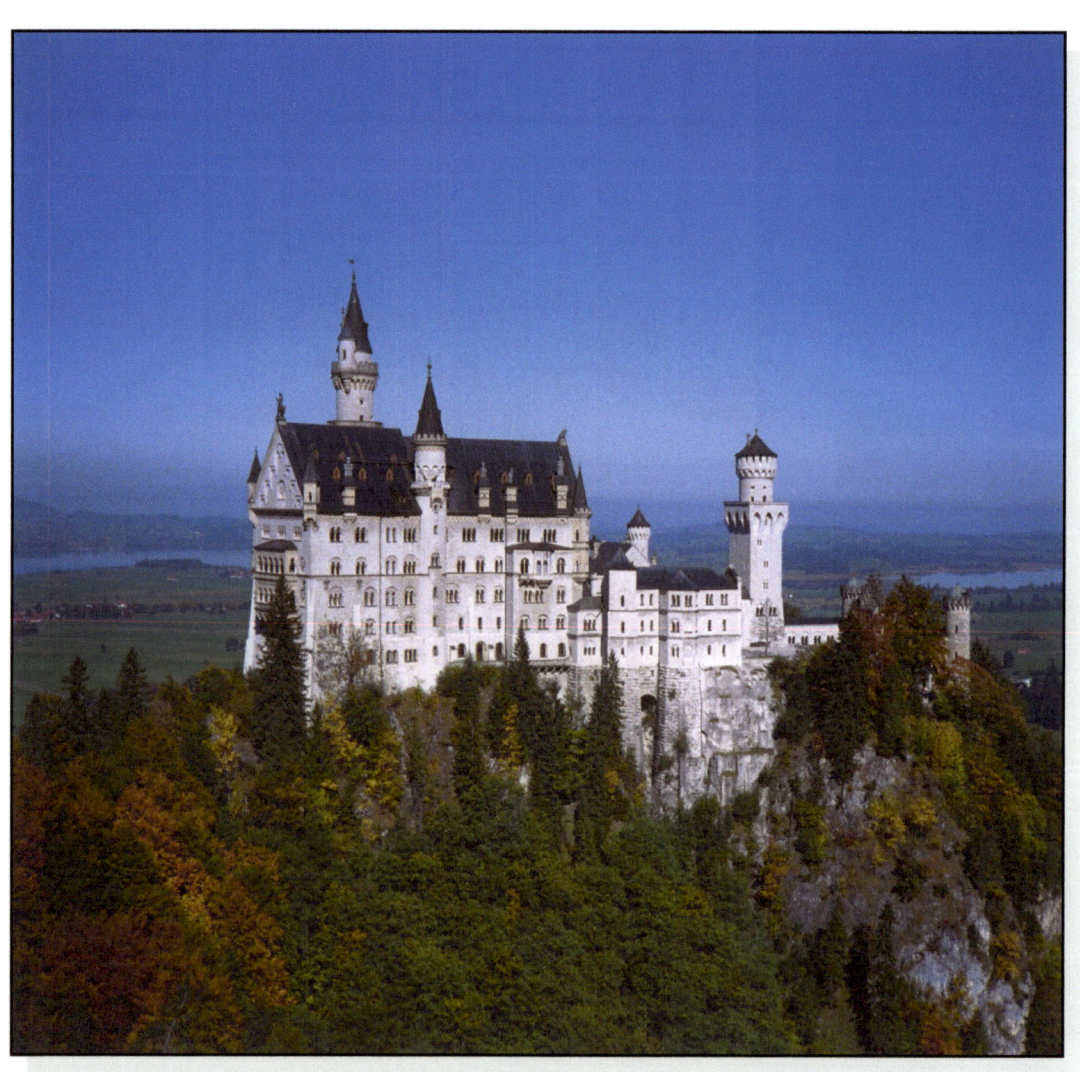

a Builder

You!

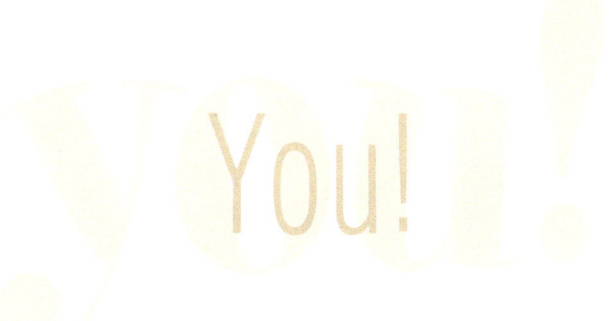

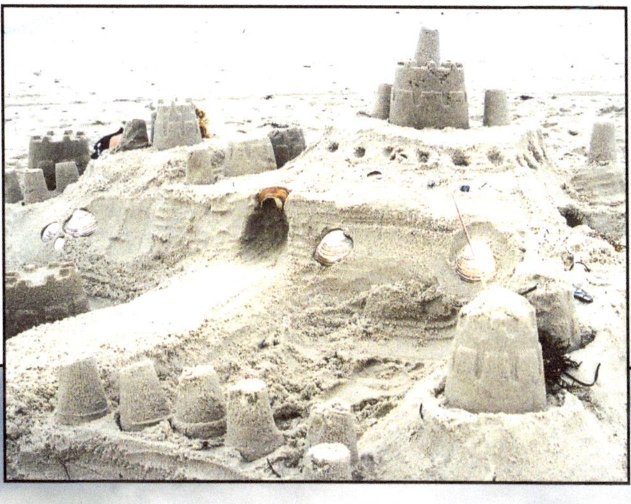

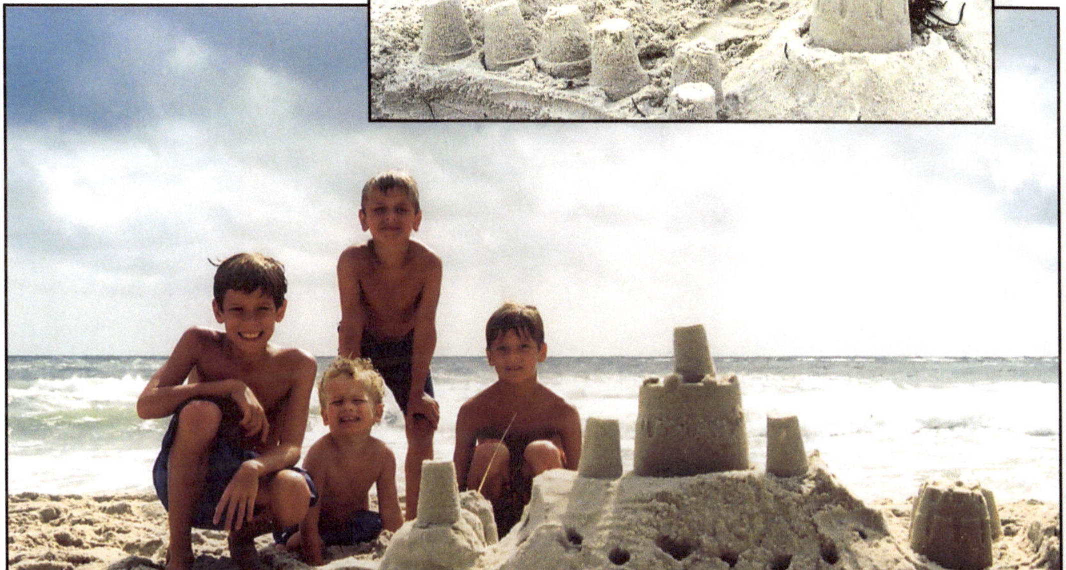

or sand.

Everyone can do art!

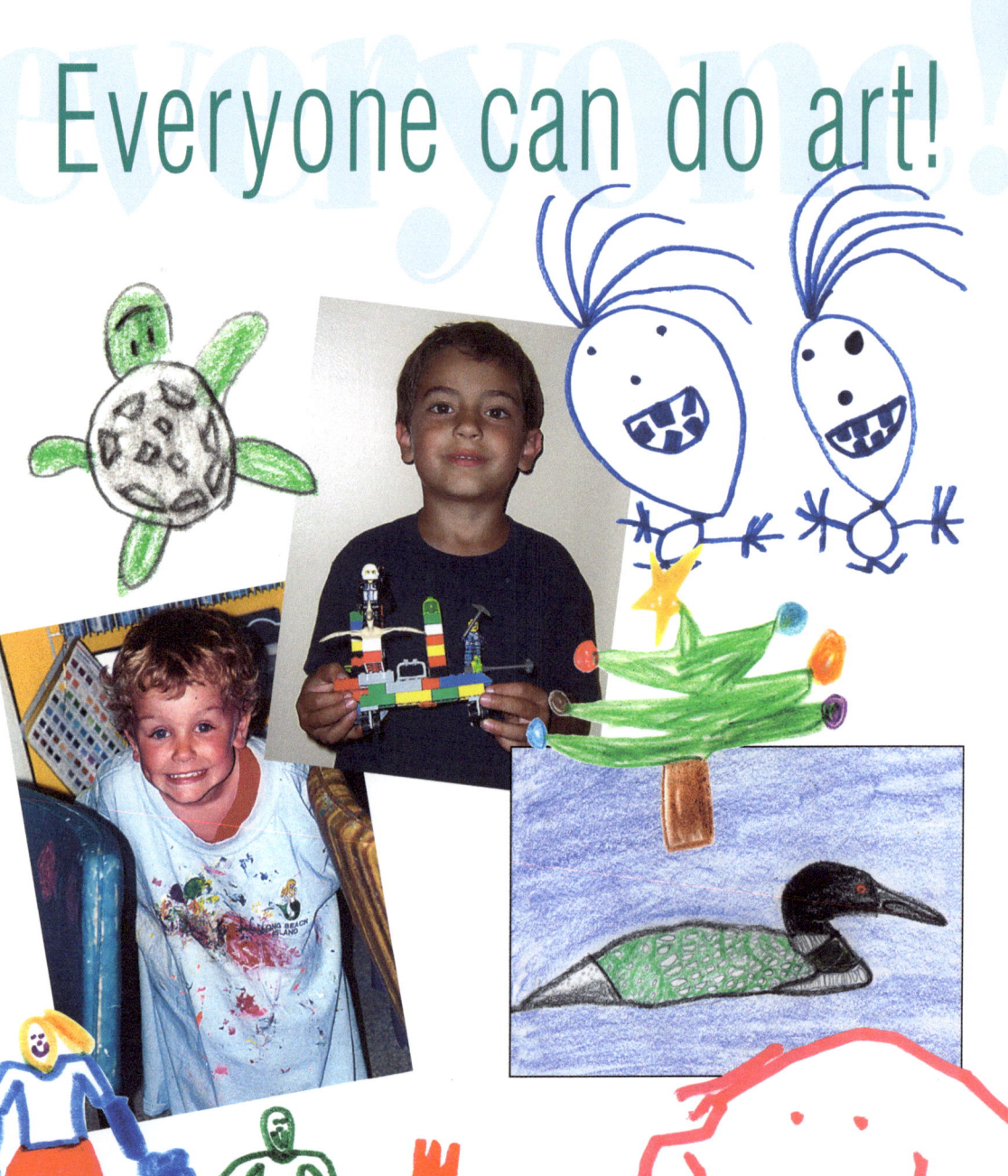

Something that's different,
that makes you smile...
is art of a kind that's just your style.

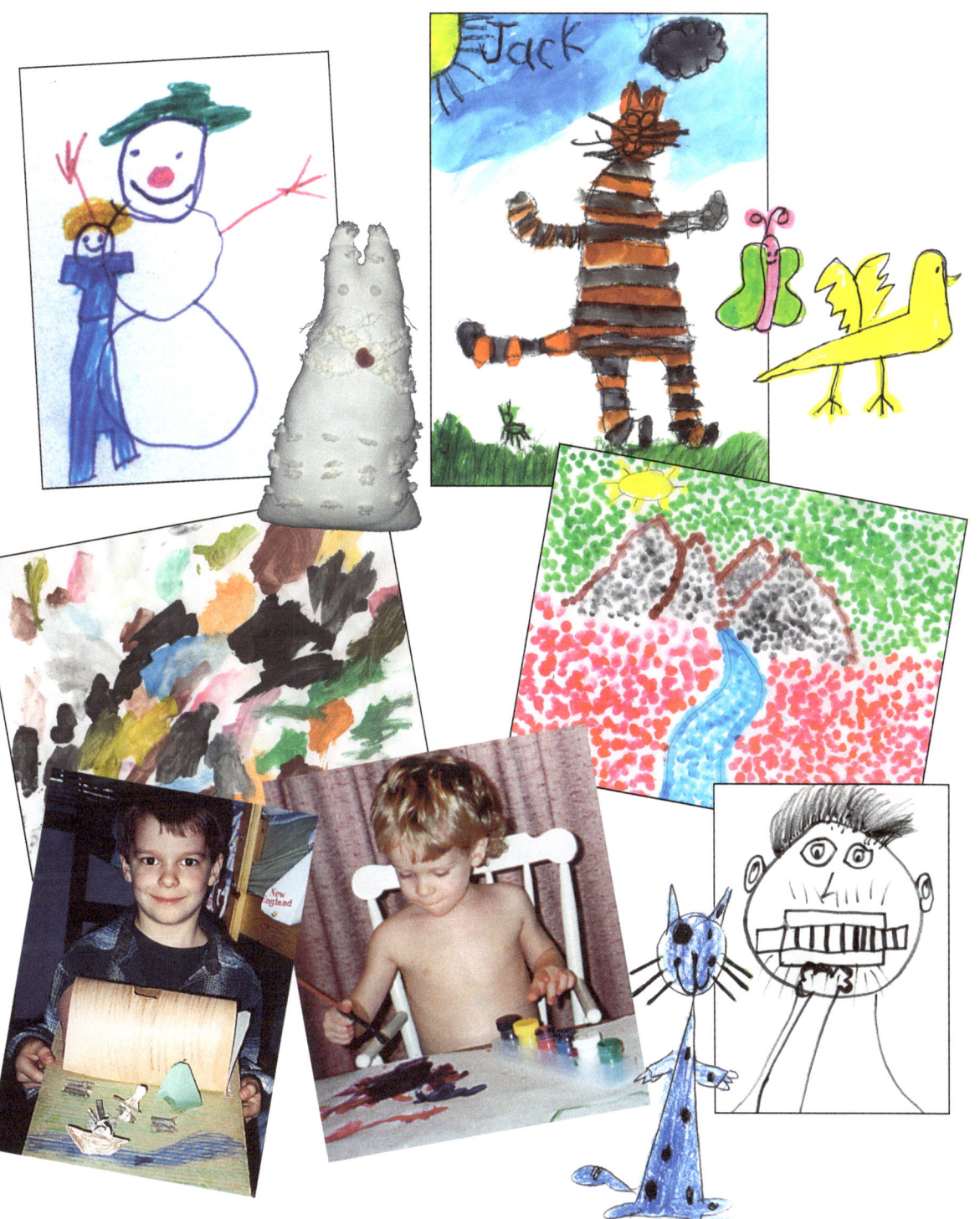

Don't think you can't do it — you *can* create art.
Let your passion guide you;
it comes from your heart.

Now it's time to do your part
and show everyone how
<u>YOU</u> CAN DO ART!